T0194023

Matcha Reimagined

A Recipe Book

Created by:

www.yangyinhealth.com

Jen Lucas & Jessica VanNewkirk

AuthorHouse™
1663 Liberty Drive
Bloomington, IN 47403
www.authorhouse.com
Phone: 1 (833) 262-8899

This book is printed on acid-free paper.

Cover image by Angela Rose Photography
https://www.thx4smiling.photos/

ISBN: 978-1-7283-6554-1 (sc)
978-1-7283-6553-4 (e)

Library of Congress Control Number: 2020912047

Print information available on the last page.

Published by AuthorHouse 09/23/2020

author HOUSE®

Introduction

Matcha, a fine, vibrant powder, is made from green tea grown primarily in China and Japan and created through a unique process that sets it apart from all other teas. The traditional method of making ordinary green tea usually involves withering, heating, rolling and drying the leaves, but this process removes some of the naturally occurring nutrients.

Matcha is the only tea in which the entire tea leaf is dissolved in the water providing the maximum benefits of natural components present in the tea, which are many. Matcha is known for its high antioxidant content, which can strengthen the immune system, but the same factor can also help to fight free radicals, which are the main cause of accelerated aging. Matcha offers a host of other health benefits such as anti-inflammatory properties that fight tooth decay, detoxifying qualities, and even UV protection. It's also loved around the world for providing balanced energy without the jitters, anxiety, or crash that some experience after drinking coffee.

While the Western world has recently caught onto the delicious powder and started using it in lattes, it has been enjoyed for centuries both in ceremonies and in preparing healthy foods and beverages. This cookbook is meant to show you a variety of ways you can include this delicious superfood in your daily life and reap all of its benefits. After all, something this good deserves to be shared.

The high-quality matcha available from Yang+Yin Health is made from the youngest tea leaves, which gives it its intense green color and delicate flavor. These qualities make it ideal for both food and beverage recipes and its high potency and nutrient content mean that a small amount goes a long way.

Inside you'll find twenty-one recipes for sweets, savory foods, drinks, and skincare that will challenge the way you look at this gorgeous green powder. They consist of simple, easy-to-find ingredients so that you don't spend more time shopping than cooking and enjoying. Each recipe provides ample options for customization and can be easily adapted to accommodate food allergies or special diets.

Now, let's get cooking.

TEA-th Love
/teTh ləv/

To spread love with a purely natural smile

 ALL-NATURAL TOOTHPASTE MADE WITH
GINGIVITIS-FIGHTING GREEN TEA EXTRACT

2oz

yang + yin
HEALTH

Mat*cha tea
/maCHə tə/

To show oneself love with
mindful, nourishing tea rituals

1.00 oz

Matcha Face Love
/maCHə fas ləv/

To provide love & natural care to one's face

A SUPERIOR, MATCHA-INFUSED
ANTI-AGING FACE CREAM

2oz

Sweet Recipes

Here you'll find a collection of recipes that showcase the complex flavors of matcha in the form of your favorite desserts and healthy treats to satisfy your sweet tooth. Go beyond store-bought snacks with these home-made, antioxidant rich bites. There's something for every sweet tooth and every occasion.

Matcha Flan

Give this classic dessert an upgrade with natural sweetener and a matcha kick. This recipe includes plating instructions to help you blow guests away.

Ingredients:

- 1 cup coconut milk
- 2 tsp agar flakes
- 2 tbsp maple syrup
- 1-1/2 tsp Y+Y organic matcha

- 1 tsp vegetable oil
- Ground sesame seeds for garnish
- Dark chocolate for garnish

Instructions:

1. Add coconut milk to a saucepan with maple syrup and agar flakes and warm over medium heat. Allow mixture to simmer just below a boil for about 3-4 minutes while stirring regularly.
2. Pour coconut mixture into a blender and add matcha. Blend on high until matcha is dissolved.
3. Rub vegetable oil on the inside of the dish for easy removal. If you don't have a small dish, try a teacup.
4. Pour mixture into the dishes. Remove bubbles by tapping dishes on the counter.
5. Refrigerate for at least 3 hours or until fully set.
6. Serve in or out of the dish. To remove from the dish scrape around the edges with a knife for easier removal.
7. Garnish with ground sesame seeds and chocolate.

Matcha Mug Cake for One

Looking to satisfy your sweet tooth without the leftovers (or dishes!) of baking a cake? You need to make this mug cake.

Ingredients:

- 1 tsp butter or butter substitute
- 1 tsp Y+Y organic matcha
- 2 tbsp honey or maple syrup
- 1 tbsp almond milk
- 1 tsp vanilla extract

- 1 egg
- Pinch of sea salt
- 1/4 cup lightly packed almond flour
- 1/8 tsp baking soda
- 1/8 tsp cream of tartar

Optional:

- 1 heaping tbsp chocolate chips

- Fresh strawberries or blueberries for topping

Directions:

1. Microwave butter until melted in mug.
2. Stir in matcha.
3. Add honey, milk, and vanilla and mix with a fork.
4. Add egg and mix again.
5. Add in almond flour, baking soda, and cream of tartar. If you are using chocolate chips, stir them in.
6. Microwave for 2 minutes. Cake should be pulling away from edges when done.
7. Let cool for at least five minutes.

Optional: Top with berries

Matcha Energy Bites

For a healthy, energy rich treat to bring on your next adventure, try out these handy morsels which feature protein-rich flaxseeds.

Ingredients:

- 1/2 cup peanut butter or almond butter
- 1/3 cup honey
- 1 tbsp coconut oil
- 1-1/2 cup old fashioned rolled oats
- 1/2 tbsp Y+Y organic matcha
- 1/2 tbsp ground flax seed
- 1/4 cup peanuts or walnuts crushed or chopped
- 1/4 cup mini chocolate chips
- 1/2 tbsp chia seeds
- 1/3 cup cocoa powder

Instructions:

1. In a small saucepan on medium-low heat, melt peanut butter, honey and coconut oil stirring constantly until combined.
2. In a bowl, combine oats, matcha, flaxseed, nuts, chocolate chips, and chia seeds.
3. Pour peanut butter mixture into oat mixture and combine.
4. Using a spring-release scoop, form balls out of the mixture.
5. Roll in cocoa powder.
6. Store in an air-tight container up to 1 week.

Matcha & Avocado Popsicle

Instead of reaching for a store-bought freezer pop full of high-fructose corn syrup and artificial coloring, keep some of these on hand. The avocado lends a smooth, creamy texture and enhances the vibrant color of the matcha, providing the cool treat you crave on hot days.

Ingredients:

Popsicle

- 2 large avocados or 3 small avocados
- 1 can coconut milk
- 2 tbsp Y+Y organic matcha
- 1 tbsp of maple syrup
- 1 tsp of pure vanilla extract

Dip for Popsicle

- 8 oz white chocolate
- 4 tbsp raw organic cacao butter

Instructions:

1. Mix popsicle ingredients in a blender at high speed until silky smooth.
2. Pour mixture in popsicle molds.
3. Insert sticks and put into the freezer overnight.

For White Chocolate Coating:

1. Chop white chocolate and melt.
2. Mix with butter until there are no lumps. Make sure chocolate is cooled but not solid.
3. Dip popsicles and hold until chocolate hardens in a few seconds. Place popsicles on a non-stick baking sheet.
4. Place back in the freezer until they set completely.
5. Wrap each popsicle in baking paper and store in a freezer tight container.

Matcha Soft Protein Bars

Much healthier than the chemical-laden protein bars found in grocery stores, these homemade versions will keep you going all day--and without the chalky aftertaste.

Ingredients:

- 1/2 cup almond butter
- 1 cup almond milk
- 1 tsp stevia extract
- 1/2 tsp vanilla extract
- 1 tsp almond extract

- 1 cup vanilla protein powder
- 2/3 cup gluten free flour
- 2 tbsp Y+Y organic matcha
- 1/8 tsp Himalayan salt

Optional: Add 1/4 cup of mini white chocolate chip and 1/4 cup of dried cranberries for a sweeter version.

Instructions:

1. Line an 8x8" pan with parchment paper.
2. In a bowl combine all ingredients. Mixture will be like cookie dough.
3. Optional: Fold in mini white chocolate chips and cranberries.
4. Scoop mixture into pan and smooth flat.
5. Tightly cover pan and refrigerate overnight.
6. Lift mixture out of the pan with parchment paper. Slice into 12 bars.

Optional: You can top the bars with sprinkled matcha or drizzled chocolate.

*Store in the refrigerator for up to 1 week or freeze.

Matcha Cream Cheese Frosting

Looking to bring the wow-factor to your next batch of baked goods? Look no further than this rich, creamy frosting.

Ingredients:

- 1/2 cup (1 stick) unsalted butter softened or vegan butter
- 8 oz cream cheese softened or vegan cream cheese
- 1 tsp vanilla extract
- 1/4 tsp salt
- 4 cups powdered sugar*
- 1 tbsp of Y+Y organic matcha

Instructions:

1. Beat butter and cream cheese with an electric mixer, until creamy and lump free.
2. Add vanilla extract and salt and continue to beat.
3. With mixer on low, gradually add powdered sugar until completely combined.
4. Once fully mixed, add matcha and blend slowly.
5. Use to frost completely cooled cake or cupcakes.

*If you plan to pipe the frosting with a small tip, we recommend sifting the powdered sugar (after measuring).

Yields enough for 24 cupcakes or a cake.

Matcha Gluten Free Muffins

This recipe brings a breakfast classic to a whole new level. Pair with a matcha latte for the perfect way to start the day.

Ingredients:

- 1-1/2 cups gluten free flour
- 3/4 cup white sugar
- 1/2 tsp salt
- 1 tbsp Y+Y organic matcha

- 2 tsp baking powder
- 1/3 cup olive oil or coconut oil
- 1 egg
- 1/3 cup almond milk

Optional:

- 1 cup fresh blueberries or $^2/_3$ cup chocolate chips or 1 cup raspberries

- Crumb topping (instructions below)

Instructions:

1. Preheat oven to 400 degrees. Grease muffin cups or line with muffin liners.
2. Combine flour, sugar, salt, matcha and baking powder. Set aside.
3. Combine oil, egg, and milk.
4. Gradually add dry mixture into wet mixture until fully combined.

To Make (optional) Crumb Topping:

1. Mix together 1/2 cup sugar, 1/3 cup flour, 1/4 cup butter, and 1 1/2 teaspoons cinnamon. Mix with fork.
2. Sprinkle over muffins before baking.
3. Bake for 20 to 25 minutes or until toothpick can be inserted and come out clean.

Yields 12 muffins.

Matcha Chia Pudding

This simple pudding recipe pairs the nutrient powerhouses of matcha and chia with comforting sweetness without overpowering the flavors of the star ingredients.

Ingredients:

- 2 cups hemp or almond milk
- 2 tbsp maple syrup (optional)
- 1 tsp vanilla extract
- 1 tsp Y+Y organic matcha
- 6 tbsp chia seeds
- dash of oj

Instructions:

1. Blend milk, maple syrup, vanilla extract, oj, and matcha together in a blender till smooth.
2. Pour liquid over the chia seeds. Stir thoroughly. Stir again every few minutes for the next twenty minutes.
3. Allow mixture to sit for at least an hour, or overnight, in the fridge.
4. Stir mixture once more, and serve with your favorite fresh fruit and/or nuts.

Yields 2 servings.

Savory Recipes

If you've only ever tasted matcha in sweets and lattes, adding it to savory dishes can seem strange, but a touch in some of your favorite foods can add a whole level of flavor and compliment other ingredients in ways you never imagined.

Vegan Matcha Pancakes

Brunch will never look the same after you introduce these vegan, gluten-free, perfect-for-topping pancakes.

Ingredients:

- 1 tbsp ground flax
- 3 tbsp water
- 1 cup soy or almond milk
- 1 tbsp apple cider vinegar
- 1 cup gluten free flour
- 2 tbsp sugar or stevia drops

- 2 tsp baking powder
- 1/2 tsp salt
- 1/2 tbsp Y+Y organic matcha
- 1-1/2 tbsp canola oil
- Cooking spray

Instructions:

1. In one bowl, whisk flax and water and set aside.
2. In another bowl, whisk milk and apple cider vinegar and set aside.
3. In a large bowl, mix flour, sugar, baking powder, salt, and matcha powder.
4. Add in canola oil.
5. Add the first two bowls. Stir everything until smooth.
6. Heat a large pan over medium heat.
7. Spray pan with cooking spray. Scoop 2 tbsp of batter into pan. Once edges begin to bubble/cook, flip the pancake.
8. Serve with your favorite toppings.

Suggested Topping Combinations:

- Toasted Coconut with Berries
- Ham & Over Easy Egg
- Sautéed Mushrooms and Scallions
- Butter & Sugar, like Sveler: a traditional Norwegian snack found on ferries
- Goat Cheese & Walnuts
- Goat Cheese & Favorite Jam
- Cinnamon Sugar Pineapples
- Sliced Avocado & Sriracha

Matcha Almond Flour Bread (Keto-friendly)

Enjoy delicious homemade bread featuring a kick of antioxidants and lacking the usual carb count.

Ingredients:

- 2 cups almond flour
- 1/4 cup psyllium husk powder
- 1 tbsp baking powder
- 1/2 tsp sea salt
- 1-1/2 tbsp Y+Y organic matcha

- 4 large eggs (beaten)
- 1/4 cup coconut oil (measured solid, then melted)
- 1/2 cup warm water

Instructions:

1. Preheat oven to 350 degrees F. Line a 9x5 inch loaf pan with parchment paper.
2. In a large bowl, stir together almond flour, psyllium husk powder, baking powder, sea salt, and matcha.
3. Stir in eggs and melted coconut oil, then finally warm water.
4. Pour batter into the baking pan. Smooth top evenly with your hands, forming a rounded top.
5. Bake for 55-70 minutes, until an inserted toothpick comes out clean and top is hard, like a bread crust. Cool completely before removing from the pan.

Pistachio Matcha Muffins

Two of your favorite green ingredients collaborate in these tasty any-time treats.

Ingredients:

- 2 tbsp ground flaxseeds
- 3/4 cup almond milk or hemp milk
- 1-1/3 cups gluten free flour
- 2 tsp baking powder
- 1 tbsp Y+Y organic matcha
- 1 tsp lemon zest
- 1 tsp cinnamon
- 1/4 tsp nutmeg
- 1/8 tsp Himalayan salt
- 1/2 cup vegan butter (room temperature)
- 1/2 cup sugar
- 2 tsp vanilla extract
- 1/2 cup chopped pistachios

Instructions:

1. Mix milk and flax seeds together in a small bowl and set aside.
2. Preheat oven to 375 F. Line 12 muffin cups with papers.
3. Combine flour, baking powder, matcha, lemon zest, cinnamon, nutmeg and salt in a large bowl. Set aside.
4. Mix butter, sugar and vanilla with a mixer in a medium bowl. Add milk/flax mixture in parts and continue mixing.
5. Add dry ingredient mixture in parts and continue mixing.
6. Spoon mixture into muffin cups.
7. Top with chopped pistachios.
8. Bake for 15 minutes or until an inserted toothpick comes out clean.

Matcha Zucchini Cakes

These summertime favorites, also known as zucchini fritters, are given an extra burst of flavor (and color) with a bit of matcha. The easily-adaptable recipe can be tailored to compliment whatever you're serving.

Ingredients:

- 2 large zucchini
- 2 large eggs
- 1/4 cup ricotta
- 1/4 cup freshly grated parmesan
- 1/2 tsp minced garlic
- 1/8 tsp cayenne pepper
- 1 tbsp Y+Y organic matcha
- Himalayan salt
- Ground black pepper
- Vegetable oil, for cooking

Instructions:

1. Use a box grater to grate zucchini. Ring out with a towel to get out excess water.
2. In a bowl combine zucchini, eggs, ricotta, parmesan, garlic, cayenne pepper, and matcha. Season with salt and pepper as needed.
3. Heat a skillet over medium heat. Add oil to come halfway up the pan. Scoop 1/4 cup of zucchini mixture into the skillet. Flatten and cook until golden brown, about 2 minutes per side.
4. Line a cutting board with paper towels and place cooked zucchini cakes on it to avoid getting greasy. Optional: You can use an air fryer instead for a healthier version.
5. Sprinkle with Himalayan salt and serve.

Cheesy Herb Matcha Biscuits

These cravable biscuits blow store bought rolls and biscuits out of the water and make a perfect appetizer or finger food at parties.

Ingredients:

- 2/3 cup of sunflower oil
- 1 large eggs
- 1-1/4 cup of buttermilk
- 4 cups self rising gluten free flour
- 1 tsp of mustard powder
- 1 bunch of scallions
- 1 bunch of snipped chives

- 1 clove of garlic, chopped
- 1 tsp Y+Y organic matcha
- 1/4 cup grated parmesan or vegan alternative
- 1 cup soft cheese diced into 1/2 inch cubes

Instructions:

1. Preheat oven to 400 degrees. Grease muffin tin or line with papers.
2. Whisk oil, egg, and buttermilk together.
3. In a separate bowl mix, flour, mustard, matcha, garlic, chives, scallion, and half of parmesan.
4. Fold wet ingredients into dry. Then, fold in cheese cubes.
5. Spoon mixture evenly into muffin tin.
6. Sprinkle remaining Parmesan on top.
7. Bake for 25 minutes or until golden brown. Let cool and serve.

Drinks

While most people are familiar to the standard, coffeehouse matcha latte, this powder's potential doesn't stop there. Combine with other natural flavors in these cold drinks and enjoy a caffeine boost along with a tasty beverage.

Matchade

When the heat has you looking for a little something extra in a cold drink, try this take on a summertime classic.

Ingredients:

- 2 quarts hot water
- 2 cups sugar
- 2 cups of lemon juice
- 2 tbsp Y+Y organic matcha

Instructions:

1. Heat up water until boiling.
2. Remove from heat and mix all ingredients until dissolved.
3. Allow mixture to cool in the refrigerator.
4. Pour over ice and enjoy.

Summer tip: Pour this into popsicle molds for a sweet treat.

Ginger Berry Matcha Smoothie

When it comes to smoothie drinks, matcha makes the perfect addition in terms of flavor, color, and nutrients.

Ingredients:

- 1 frozen banana
- 1 cup almond milk
- 2 tsp Y+Y organic matcha
- 1/2 cup of spinach
- 1/4 cup of blueberries
- 1/4 cup of strawberries
- 1/2 tsp grated ginger
- Handful of ice

Instructions:

1. Add all ingredients, put ice into the blender. Mix until smooth.
2. Add ice until desired thickness.

Rose Matcha Latte

Upgrade this beloved standard with a floral complement and summertime twist.

Ingredients:

- 1/2 cup water
- 1 tsp Y+Y organic matcha
- 3/4 cup almond milk
- 3 tbsp rose hibiscus concentrate
- Ice
- Optional: honey

Instructions:

1. Boil water until boiling point.
2. Remove from heat and whisk in matcha.
3. Put matcha in the refrigerator until cool.
4. In a shaker, combine milk and rose concentrate.
5. Pour rose mixture over ice.
6. Pour cooled matcha tea on top and enjoy.

Matcha & Mint

Refreshing, flavorful, and light, this drink hits all the marks after a day in the sun.

Ingredients:

- 2 cups water
- 2 tsp Y+Y organic matcha
- 2 cups crushed ice
- 1 sliced lime
- Handful of mint
- Optional: honey

Instructions:

1. Combine water and matcha in a cocktail shaker.
2. Add ice, a squeeze of lime, and mint and continue shaking. (Honey is optional.)
3. Pour into glasses. Garnish with a lime wedge.

Variations: This is the perfect base for your mojito recipe. Just swap the water for club soda and add Rum.

Skincare Recipes

In addition to it's amazing nutritional factors, matcha offers a host of benefits to the skin, such as anti-inflammatory properties which help to smooth fine lines. This makes it an excellent alternative to the chemicals found in many skincare products.

Matcha Facial Cleanser

Use this simple cleanser right before bed to clear out pores and soothe dry skin, as tea tree oil combines with matcha for moisturizing benefits.

Ingredients:

- 4 tbsp organic honey
- 4 tbsp sunflower oil
- 4 tbsp unscented castile soap
- 1 tbsp Y+Y organic matcha
- 5 drops tea tree essential oil
- 10 drops of lavender essential oil
- Water
- 8 oz bottle container

Instructions:

1. Fill the bottle with all ingredients except water.
2. Fill remaining space in the bottle with water.

*Shake before every use.

Sensitive Skin Matcha Facial Toner

Get smooth, even skin without experimenting with questionable chemicals. This simple recipe does the job and can be made at home in minutes.

Ingredients:

- 1-1/2 ounces apple cider vinegar
- 1-1/2 ounces witch hazel
- 5 ounces water
- 5 drops of tea tree essential oil
- 5 drops of lavender essential oil
- 1/4 tsp Y+Y organic matcha

Instructions:

1. Mix all ingredients until well combined.
2. Pour into an 8 ounce spray bottle.

* Shake before every use.

Matcha Sugar Scrub

Treat your skin to this sweet scrub that gently exfoliates, leaving your skin smooth and glowing.

Ingredients:

- 1 tsp of Y+Y organic matcha
- 1/2 cup of organic safflower oil or sunflower oil
- 1 cup of sugar
- 10 drops of bergamot essential oil
- 10 drops of lime essential oil
- Jars for storing

Instructions:

1. Whisk oil and matcha.
2. Add essential oils and continue mixing.
3. Fold sugar into oil mixture.
4. Pour into a water-tight container.

* Store extra jars in the fridge if they will be used at a later date. Yields about one 8 oz container. Caution: Oil can cause the bathtub to be slippery.

For sensitive skin, switch bergamot and lime essential oils for chamomile and lavender essential oils.

Matcha Acne Spot Treatment RollerBall

Tackle spots with this powerhouse combination of essential oils and matcha conveniently applied with a cosmetic roller.

Ingredients:

- 1 tsp of frankincense essential oil
- 1 tsp lavender essential oil
- 1 tsp tea tree essential oil
- 1/4 tsp Y+Y organic matcha
- 1/4 cup of almond oil or sunflower oil

Instructions:

1. Mix all ingredients in a glass.
2. Gently pour into roller balls.

* Yields about 6-7 roller balls. Shake before every use.

The perfect ingredient available for

purchase at www.yangyinhealth.com

Printed in the United States
By Bookmasters